THOSE
DARING MACHINES

# JEEP™

by
Peter Guttmacher

Crestwood House
New York

Maxwell Macmillan Canada
Toronto

Maxwell Macmillan International
New York   Oxford   Singapore   Sydney

**Library of Congress Cataloging-in-Publication Data**
Guttmacher, Peter.
    Jeep / by Peter Guttmacher. — 1st ed.
      p.   cm. — (Those daring machines)
    Includes index.
    Summary: Traces the history of the rugged American all-purpose vehicle the Jeep from its creation
as a war machine to its popularity on roads today.
    ISBN 0-89686-830-3
    1. Jeep automobile — History — Juvenile literature. [1. Jeep automobile — History.] I. Title. II. Series.
    TL215.J44G88 1994
    629.222'2 — dc20                            93-10476

3 9082 05626045 1

Crestwood House
Macmillan Publishing Company
866 Third Avenue
New York, NY 10022

Maxwell Macmillan Canada, Inc.
1200 Eglinton Avenue East
Suite 200
Don Mills, Ontario M3C 3N1

Macmillan Publishing Company is part of the Maxwell Communication Group of Companies

First Edition

Printed in the United States of America

10 9 8 7 6 5 4 3 2 1


**Created and Developed by The Learning Source**


### Acknowledgments

We would like to thank the many people who helped with this book. Special thanks are owed to Mike Aberlich and all the other people at the Jeep Division of Chrysler Corporation. Without them none of this would have been possible.

Jeep™ is a trademark of the Chrysler Corporation.

**Photo Credits**
Chrysler Corporation: cover (top, center), pp. 12, 15, 20, 24, 26, 28, 29, 31, 35, 37, 43; Delaney Films: 4, 39, 42; Detroit Public Library: pp. 13, 16, 19, 25; Ford Motor Company: p. 8; Jim Frenak/Media Creations: cover (lower), pp. 36, 40; Philippine Department of Tourism: p. 22.

# CONTENTS

# CREATURES IN THE WILD

I magine this. You're mountain climbing miles from nowhere in California's Sierra Nevada. Or perhaps you're in a hot Arizona desert canyon or on the shores of any icy lake in Maine. Wherever you may be, imagine that dusk is upon you. The sun is slipping out of sight. Night in the wild is coming to life.

Listen closely. You might hear more than the moan of the wind or the howl of a coyote. You might hear an odd roaring and scrambling that reaches your ears from deep in the wilderness.

For half a century those weird sounds have come from a pack of unstoppable creatures. You might spot them crawling along ancient trails once used by the Apache or the Cherokee. These creatures have been sighted on old stagecoach roads, screaming past ghost towns and now-empty gold mines. On steep or rocky ground they move slowly. But any one of them can run faster than a mountain lion and leap almost as well as a mountain goat.

Jeeps can climb just
about anything!

Each of these creatures can pull itself over huge boulders or slabs of rock and claw its way out of mud-filled ditches. It can charge over a hilltop and then fly through the air and smash down on all fours – without missing a beat.

These fierce beings have fought terrible enemies and left their tracks across deserts, jungles, swamps, and snowfields. Some have raced away on missions of mercy, carrying the dead and wounded from battlefields. One has even tried to swim the Atlantic Ocean.

These amazing creatures have somehow drawn millions of people into places seldom visited before. Watch out! You could be next.

Have you guessed what this astonishing creature is? No, it's not Bigfoot or the Loch Ness monster. Nor is it the Abominable Snowman on the loose. Here's how a dictionary might define this amazing creature:

> A small, rugged automotive vehicle, with a one-quarter-ton capacity. It has **four-wheel drive** and can carry four people or three people and a machine gun. It was first used by U.S. armed forces in World War II.

This mouthful of words can be chewed down to one amazing machine. This unstoppable object is perhaps the most famous car in history. Its name is J-E-E-P.

# THE JEEP IS BORN

*Jeep was a universal idea which no one invented, created, or developed.*
—General J. W. Curtis

Almost as soon as the automobile was invented, the U.S. Army started looking for a way to use cars to move troops and supplies over the battlefield. It was only logical that the army would want to take advantage of the new invention and trade in its horses and mules for motorized vehicles. After all, animals had to be fed, calmed, and sheltered. And machines didn't die of exhaustion or sickness the way animals did. Nor did the machines buck at the sound of gunfire.

Finding the right vehicle for wartime, however, was a challenge. By 1897, for example, the French army had tried adding motors to tricycles and quadricycles. Great Britain was testing vehicles for war, too. But most of these vehicles were too weak and too clumsy to make their way across war-torn land.

After World War I ended, in 1918, the U.S. armed forces tried some experiments. In 1921 they took the wheels off a vehicle and fitted it with two big belts, like those on a tank. The vehicle was not a success.

Two years later the army stripped down a Model T Ford until it was just a frame, a motor, and four wheels. This lightened vehicle performed well, but its small tires sank in the mud. So the army took off those tires and put on airplane tires. To the army's delight, its new vehicle could even drive across a swamp without getting stuck.

The Ford Model T, shown here, was a family car, but a stripped-down version later became a military vehicle.

In 1939, war broke out in Europe once again. At the time, the U.S. Army was using two basic vehicles. Neither was exactly right for war. The first of these was a motorcycle with a sidecar, a small, wheeled shell. These machines were fast—mainly because they could carry only a couple of people. But they could carry little else. And they made enough noise to wake the dead. What's more, a big bump or pothole could send everything flying— motorcycle, sidecar, people, and all.

Trucks were the army's other main vehicle. They were great for moving soldiers and supplies. But they were big. And they tended to get stuck in mud, snow, and sand. They also were so slow that they made easy targets for enemy gunners.

What the army needed was something between these two machines in size. The new vehicle had to be big and strong enough to transport at least some equipment. It had to be small enough to move quickly under enemy fire. It also had to be stable enough to scramble over rocks and rough ground. And it had to have enough **traction** to scoot through just about anything—rocks, mud, snow, or even ice. But who was going to invent a machine that could meet all these requirements?

An army sergeant named Melvyn C. Wiley gave it a try. He started with ideas given to him by Colonel Robert G.

Howie. Wiley then experimented until he invented the "Howie Bellyflopper." If nothing else, the Bellyflopper was different. It was a low, four-wheeled platform only inches off the ground. Drivers lay on their stomachs and steered with their feet. This position left their hands free to use the rifle that was mounted on the front.

The little Bellyflopper was exciting—and cute. But it had real problems. Even though it was close to the ground, the machine didn't hold the road well. Nor did it have any shock absorbers. A few hours on the Bellyflopper would make anyone want to rename it the *Backbreaker*. Still, the Bellyflopper had one important thing going for it. It was so close to the ground that it made a difficult target for enemy guns.

The Bellyflopper set the army thinking. What if some actual car builders were asked to make a vehicle for the armed forces? Could *they* come up with a good solution?

CHAPTER

3

# CALLING ALL CARS...

**M**essages went out to 135 American car manufacturers. The army needed what it called a "low-
silhouette scout car," a vehicle that was small
and close to the ground. In fact, the army asked that it
be no more than 3 feet off the ground.

The new vehicle had to be able to carry weapons and
handle a long list of other jobs. The army also said that the
car must weigh no more than 1,300 pounds—much less
than most cars of that time. And it had to be able to pull
more than 500 pounds.

The new car would also need to have four-wheel-drive.
In most cars built in the 1940s, power from the motor
turned the rear wheels. The rear wheels then pushed
the front wheels—and the whole car—along. This
system worked fine under most conditions. But not when
the cars ran into mud, snow, ice, or even deep sand.
Their wheels tended to spin on ice or snow and get stuck
in mud or sand.

The Willys Quad arrived for tests in 1940.

With a four-wheel-drive system, engine power goes to all four wheels. This means that four-wheel-drive vehicles have a better chance of getting through snow or mud—and of getting across ice or rough, rocky ground.

Last of all, the army needed the new cars in a hurry. The first model would have to be delivered in 49 days. Seventy more vehicles had to be received 75 days later.

Only two automakers answered the army's call. The "rush" nature of the project probably had a lot to do with this. Also, most car manufacturers probably felt that there wasn't much money in the business of making vehicles for the army. After all, what if the United States didn't enter the war? A peacetime army probably wouldn't need many vehicles at all. And even if there was a war, what would happen afterward? The fashion of the time was for long, wide, heavy cars. What civilian would want to drive as small and strange-looking a vehicle as the one the army called for?

The two companies that did send in designs were Willys-Overland Motors, Inc. and the American Bantam Car Company. Willys-Overland was a large car manufacturer based in Toledo, Ohio. Bantam was a more modest company in Butler, Pennsylvania. It was known for making small cars that gave great gas mileage (up to 45 miles per gallon). Both companies believed that they could make money from the army's vehicle.

Bantam had its car ready first. The car's designer carefully drove the first vehicle to Camp Holabird, in Maryland, for testing. He had to be there by five o'clock. He went slowly and gently at first. Only when the deadline drew near did he push the car to top speed.

The army tested all models in the very toughest conditions.

Army drivers, however, were not so gentle. They tested this—and other Bantam models—in sand traps, over log roads, and into a 300-foot mud pit. Then they flew the cars off a 4-foot-high loading platform at 30 miles per hour.

After 3,400 miles of this kind of torture, is it any surprise that the Bantam cars developed a few problems? Taillights fell off, **differentials** quit working, and **axles** broke down. Frames cracked, too. But all in all, the Bantam cars had done very well. The army was impressed.

Meanwhile, Willys-Overland was hard at work. In fact, the company was building two different vehicles. One of them steered, like most cars and trucks, with only the front wheels. The other was a new, more exciting design. It steered with all four wheels. It was meant to move more quickly and easily than other vehicles.

Tests of the Willys-Overland vehicles began in November 1940. Like the Bantam machines, the Willys-Overland vehicles had a few **bugs**. But army officials liked these cars, especially their strong, powerful engines.

The army now could choose between vehicles from two different manufacturers. Still, a number of high-ranking officers were not satisfied. Bantam, they felt, was too small to produce the number of vehicles the army would need. The officers wanted a big, experienced company to get involved in the project.

They soon got their wish. Not long after the army finished testing the Bantam cars, the Ford Motor Company suggested that it might want to provide a vehicle, too. The army's problem was solved. After all, Ford was the company that had produced the Model T, the car that "put America on wheels." Who could know more than Ford about building small, inexpensive cars by the thousands?

Now it was time for the army to choose the best design. To be fair—and to get the best possible vehicle for its soldiers—the army ordered 1,500 cars from each of the three companies. This process would give the army plenty of vehicles to test.

At the same time, though, the army set new, even tougher standards for their car. This time, the vehicles would have to be able to get up to 55 miles an hour—and creep along at not more than 3 miles an hour. They would also have to be able to carry 800 pounds of people and equipment . . . and cross through 18 inches of water without suffering any damage.

There was another important change as well. The army had learned several things from its tests. First, the car needed a powerful engine, one like the engine from Willys-Overland. An engine like this was heavy. But there was no way the car would be a success without it.

Second, the car had to be strong enough to survive even the worst conditions. That meant added pieces, stronger metal, and even more weight. So the army scrapped the old 1,300 pound limit. Two-wheel steering vehicles could now weigh up to 2,100 pounds. Four-wheel steering machines had a limit of 2,175 pounds.

The three companies went back to work. From the first, the Willys-Overland engine gave the company an advantage. But it also gave the engineers a major problem —weight. The Willys-Overland design was seriously

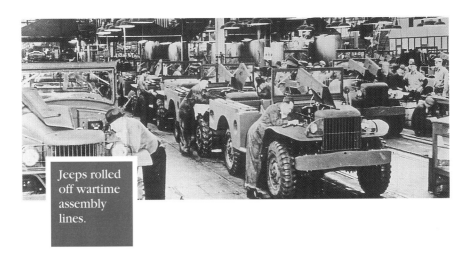

Jeeps rolled off wartime assembly lines.

overweight. In fact, it was more than 250 pounds over the limit. So the company's chief engineer, Barney Roos, put the car on a serious diet.

Mechanics took the vehicles apart, piece by piece, looking for ways to cut weight. Wherever they could, they used steel that was lighter but just as strong. They cut bolts shorter and made parts smaller. They even weighed the paint and spread it more thinly. Finally, the **Quad**, as the engineers called the four-wheel-drive car, squeaked by with just 7 ounces to spare. It was so close to the limit, one army officer joked, that Willys-Overland needed to keep the cars very clean. After all, it would not take much dust or dirt to disqualify them.

Willys's decision to keep its engine as it was paid off. The army chose the Quads for the car's basic design. But the army did not want to be tied to only one supplier. After all, what would happen if enemy attacks or **sabotage** knocked out the only factory supplying the new vehicles? To protect itself, the army wanted two companies making the Willys Quads. So it asked Ford to pitch in and build some of the cars, too.

Soon both companies were turning out vehicles. And, in time, even the little Bantam company was building Willys-designed cars. By war's end, in August 1945, the three companies had produced more than 900,000 vehicles.

## CUSTOM JEEPING

Early jeeps were simple and, in most ways, practical. The small, open-air vehicles were well-known for getting around and doing their job. Every built-in feature had a purpose. For example, there were hooks attached to the back for hanging hospital stretchers. Headlights could swivel in all directions, including backward. This gave soldiers light in the dead of night, even for working on their own vehicles. But still, with all these features, there were no luxuries or comforts in a jeep.

*Basic* was the best word for describing early jeeps. First of all, they had no heaters. In winter, jeeps were so cold that soldiers called them pneumonia wagons. Front fenders were merely slabs of metal. So dirt, mud, and even stones were sprayed everywhere. Windshield wipers worked by hand, not by motor. And to change from two- to four-wheel drive, a driver had to stop, get out, and lock the **hubs** on the front axles.

It is not surprising that soldiers and mechanics constantly looked for ways to make their jeeps more livable and lovable. Changing a jeep to suit your own personality became a popular army pastime. Some changes were ridiculously simple. Others were simply ridiculous.

Army mechanics found clever ways to direct hot air from the engine to the area around the front seat. The smell was awful, but it did keep people from freezing. Some soldiers used wood or canvas to enclose the open sides and make a roof. Another interesting "roof" came from the cockpit glass of a B-17 bomber. Soldiers would also fit a huge **poncho** over the heads of the driver and all three passengers. These home-built systems helped keep soldiers warm and dry. But they certainly made emergency **bailouts** difficult.

*Basic* was the word for the insides of early jeeps.

A ride in a jeep could be fairly miserable. One war correspondent reported that it was a moving experience, indeed. "I survived a 150-mile tour in a jeep," he wrote. But, he explained, it took "24 hours to stop vibrating" afterward.

Many soldiers made the ride more comfortable by outfitting their jeeps with pillows. Even General George

Patton, one of the army's best-known tough guys, had red leather cushions in the passenger seat of his jeep.

The jeep's fold-down windshield also led to trouble. Soldiers had to lower the windshield in order to fire a gun straight ahead. So most drivers on the front lines drove with their windshields down. Enemy soldiers knew this and strung razor-sharp wire across the trails used by the jeeps. Many soldiers were wounded, and some even were decapitated, by these deadly traps.

Soldiers quickly took action to protect themselves. The simplest solution was an upright metal bar welded onto

Jeeps could cross streams and shallow rivers on their way into battle.

the front of a jeep. The bar cut through the wire before an injury could occur.

Soldiers even found ways to waterproof jeeps so the machines could be driven through shallow ponds or rivers. Mechanics began the waterproofing process by attaching **snorkels**, or long tubes, to a jeep's engine. These carried air and exhaust in and out of the engine. Then grease was smeared all over the engine to protect it from moisture. In this way a jeep could last in the water for about eight minutes, enough time to drive across most shallow rivers. Waterproof jeeps could even tow floating trailers when more supplies had to be moved.

When "wading" wasn't enough, jeeps were made to swim. By 1941 yacht designer Roderic Stephens, Jr., was working on a machine called the general purpose **amphibian.** (An amphibian is a creature that can live on both land and water.) Soldiers quickly nicknamed Stephens's invention the **seep**.

Over 7,000 seeps hit the water in April 1942. Their metal parts were filled with air, which helped them float. Big, balloon tires helped, too. A rudder was attached to the steering wheel, so the seep could be navigated in water. A propeller made the seep go backward and forward. And, of course, every seep had an anchor.

The biggest problem was getting a seep out of the water and onto the land. On anything but a gently sloping bank, a seep tended to slide back down into the water. This limited its usefulness. But still, seeps proved helpful in many situations during the war. And, in the years following the war, seeps often found jobs doing rescue work in floods and other disasters.

Armor was another addition to the gear of many basic jeeps. Where fighting was heaviest, soldiers welded iron or steel plates over the windshields. Then they cut narrow slots so they could see ahead and aim their machine guns.

Machine guns were mounted on jeeps almost from the beginning. But the vehicles were soon rigged for bigger weapons. By 1944, **mortars** (short cannons) and **rockets** were being hung on the sides of jeeps. In time, jeeps even carried antiaircraft guns and towed antitank guns.

This Philippine taxi is made up of World War II jeep parts.

By the end of World War II, there seemed to be little that these rough-and-tumble vehicles couldn't do. All it took to put them to work was creative energy and the time to experiment.

# JEEPS ON THE JOB

Where did jeeps go and what did they do during the war? The answer is, just about everywhere and everything. By 1942, U.S. troops weren't the only ones using jeeps. Great Britain, France, the Soviet Union, and other countries were ordering them as well.

In 1942, jeeps proved themselves in the jungles of Burma (the country that now is called Myanmar). There, Americans were helping the British and Chinese defend Burma from Japanese invaders. The enemy swept in from neighboring Thailand, and the Americans and their allies had no choice but to retreat. They made their way, through hundreds of miles, to India.

Jeeps went ahead to scout paths through the thick jungle. Jeeps also hauled trucks through streams and up steep slopes. There were no real roads for the jeeps to use. But that didn't stop them. Neither did rows of high dirt ridges. The jeeps just backed up, gathered speed, and sailed over the bumps, like hurdlers in a track meet.

Jeeps were just as valuable in North Africa's Sahara desert. There their color was changed from green to brown to help hide them in the desert sand. Jeeps were also equipped with screens that kept sand out of the engines. Extra water tanks were added to cool the engines. Finally, the jeeps were packed to the limit with weapons, armor, and extra gas cans. After all, soldiers certainly couldn't count on finding many gas stations in the sand dunes of the Sahara.

Jeeps tackled the tough Burma Road.

One of the jeeps' most daring missions came in 1942. The British Eighth Army sent a commando force, in jeeps, sweeping behind enemy lines. One night, the commandos spotted a convoy of German trucks carrying fuel for the tanks of General Erwin Rommel's Afrika Korps.

The jeeps proved to be the perfect attack vehicles. The jeeps quickly grouped themselves into a wedge formation. Then they came roaring in at full speed, firing every weapon they had. The entire convoy—and a whole shipment of fuel—was destroyed. It was a smashing victory for the jeeps. And it helped lead to the defeat of the Germans in North Africa.

In North Africa, jeeps even took on tanks, though never one on one. Instead they swarmed the heavy armored vehicles. As one soldier said, "It's like **David and Goliath**, only there are ten Davids for every Goliath."

Throughout the war, jeeps were used for rescue as well as for battle. In the Battle of the Bulge, toward the end of the war in Europe, jeeps worked as ambulances. Stretchers were mounted on the backs and middles of the vehicles. Stretchers were even put over the hoods. Despite the added weight, the jeeps still managed to speed the wounded to medical care.

Rafts easily carried lightweight jeeps across deep rivers.

Army jeeps line up, from the 1940 MA to the recent M38A1.

Jeeps were equally at home in snow. They made their way through snowfields in places from Alaska to Iceland. They also kept roads plowed and airfields clear. Normally, knobby tires and their built-in four-wheel traction were all the jeeps needed to get the job done. But when the snow was deep, jeeps could always go skiing. Snowbound soldiers simply fitted their jeeps with **Caterpillar tracks** in back and skis in front.

## WHAT'S IN A NAME?

**P**eople still argue about how the jeep got its strange name. Over the years the vehicle was also nicknamed Peep, Beep, Beetle Bug, Leaping Lena, and Puddle Jumper. But somehow the name *jeep* seemed to stick.

Some people claim that the vehicle was named after a character from the Popeye comic strip and cartoons. Eugene the Jeep was a strange, magical character from that series. He came from Africa and ate nothing but **orchids.** When he was not eating flowers, Eugene would solve problems—or even answer questions about the future. Then he would disappear to who-knows-where until the next difficulty arose.

Other people believe that the word *jeep* was a blend of the sounds heard in the term *G.P.*, which stood for *general purpose*. The jeep was, after all, a general purpose vehicle.

Still other people feel that jeep was army slang for anything that had not yet proven itself. New soldiers were called jeeps; so were untested pieces of equipment.

Although people can't agree where the name came from, they do know when it reached the public. In 1941, Willys-Overland took a test jeep to Washington, D.C., to show it off. A reporter for the *Washington Post* newspaper was there for the occasion. The jeep's driver called his new vehicle a jeep, and the name went straight into print. The *Post* headline ran, "JEEP CREEPS UP CAPITOL STEPS." The rest, as they say, is history.

In 1946 the first civilian jeep was launched.

By 1946 World War II had ended, and Willys-Overland had big plans for its little car. Cars were in short supply in America. Thousands and thousands of jeep lovers—homecoming American soldiers—were on their way back from overseas. Who wouldn't want one of these wonderful wartime heroes, especially if it was cheap and didn't use a lot of gasoline? All of this led Willys-Overland to believe that jeeps would be a smashing success during peacetime.

Changes were made. Cushions were put on the seats for comfort, and the cars were painted colors other than green and brown. Motors were added to operate the windshield wipers. There was even a special attachment that turned jeeps into excellent farm machines. The same jeep that

# Discover how useful a car can be

## 'Jeep' Station Wagon

**NO WONDER** 'Jeep' Station Wagon owners marvel at their gas mileage! At speeds above 30, an overdrive cuts engine speed 30%, traveling you 42% farther for every turn of the engine.

**WITH SEATS REMOVED,** you have 98 cubic feet of load space, more with the tailgate lowered. Seats and interior are washable. It's a truly useful car, with double utility for greater value.

Talk to 'Jeep' Station Wagon owners to discover how useful a car can be—how economical and all-around satisfying.

They'll tell you it's grand for families—a comfortable passenger car, with upholstery children won't harm . . . and, with seats out, a practical vehicle for hauling, too.

Women will tell you how easily it handles, how smoothly it rides on rough roads. Men will brag on mileage and low maintenance.

See it now at Willys-Overland dealers— the *first* station wagon with an all-steel body.

THE NEW *'Jeep' Station Sedan* is an entirely new type of car . . . giving you the spaciousness of a station wagon and the luxurious comfort of a sedan. There is unusual leg and head room for six in its all-steel body, plus a large, accessible luggage space. Its new Willys-Overland '6' Engine, with overdrive, gives smooth performance, together with remarkable gasoline mileage. You'll like everything about it, including its smart styling.

Ads introduced the 1946 jeep station wagon to the public.

carried a farmer to town could also cut hay, drill wells, saw wood, and even dig holes for fence posts.

Between 1946 and 1948, Willys-Overland introduced several new jeeplike vehicles. There were comfortable station wagons and delivery sedans. There were two-wheel-drive and four-wheel-drive pickup trucks and, finally, the Jeepster Sports Phaeton, the company's first off-road fun car.

The problem was that Willys was way ahead of its time. It would be at least 20 more years before off-road recreation vehicles (RVs, as they are called today) became popular. Although some people bought jeeps, sales, in general, were disappointing.

In 1948 another problem arose. Willys-Overland was sued over its claims to have created the jeep. The company had bragged a lot in its advertisements after the war. Americans believed that jeeps had just about won the war. And most people thought that Willys-Overland had invented the jeep. Understandably, the American Bantam Car Company was angry. After all, the early Bantam machine had directly influenced Willys-Overland's design.

The Federal Trade Commission carefully considered the facts. Then it ruled that the idea for the jeep had come from the army and Bantam. Willys-Overland was ordered to stop claiming that the jeep was its brainstorm.

Other legal hassles arose and did not stop until June 1950. That was when Willys-Overland was able to take complete ownership of the famous jeep name. With that, the name was trademarked, and, thereafter, a jeep would always be a Jeep.

As the years passed, the vehicles continued to change and improve. But Jeeps did not catch on as much as Willys-Overland had hoped. In 1953 Henry J. Kaiser (of Kaiser Passenger Cars) bought Willys-Overland for a whopping $60 million. He had the wisdom to leave well enough alone. Kaiser changed nothing about the company but its name. It now was called the Willys Motor Company.

In 1955 the new company made one of the most popular Jeeps ever. The new CJ5 was made for **civilians.** But it was based on the army's M38A1 vehicle, a machine that was used in the Korean War. The M38A1 was so good that the army kept right on using it—almost unchanged—right on up to 1983. The CJ5 was a lot like the army's machine. The seats were softer, however, and the car looked a bit less like a box on wheels.

All through the 1950s, Kaiser had two main goals for Jeeps. The first was to discover why the Jeep hadn't quite caught on with the public. The other was to sell and manufacture Jeeps in foreign countries. Eventually both goals would be achieved. But at the time, Jeeps tended to be bought by people with different—or even unusual—ideas.

# THE JEEP CRAZE FINALLY TAKES OFF

By 1962 Henry J. Kaiser's Willys Motor Company came up with the design that would finally win fans for the Jeep all across the United States. It was the J line of Wagoneer station wagons and Gladiator pickups. These vehicles combined four-wheel drive with an automatic transmission. The exterior was more attractive than anything seen on a Jeep before. Just as important, the engine was more powerful, and the car was easier to drive.

Then, in 1965, the CJ5 and CJ6 Jeep Universal got new engines. With six cylinders, these new engines doubled the 72 horsepower of the old Hurricane motor that had powered Jeeps for years. That year the new Super-Wagoneer won prizes at several important auto shows. Jeep popularity was on the rise, and by 1969 the Willys Motor Company was making Jeeps for sale in 150 foreign countries.

Jeep was growing, but it was getting too big for a midsize carmaker. In 1970 the American Motors

Corporation bought Jeep from Kaiser for $70 million. Within ten years American Motors increased production from 175 to 700 Jeeps a day.

What was behind the Jeep's new popularity? For one thing, modern household appliances were saving Americans from dozens of boring chores each week and giving people hours of free time. With all this time on their hands, many Americans wanted to do something exciting and different—perhaps even have an adventure or two.

With a Jeep, a family could set out for new places—along beaches, through snow, across deserts, and even over mountain trails. It was a way to escape from the everyday world, to go anywhere and do almost anything. Perhaps that's why American Motors gave many of the new Jeeps rough-and-tough names like Commando, Renegade, Scrambler, and Wrangler.

When the United States celebrated its 200th birthday, in 1976, American Motors introduced the seventh generation of the Jeep. A memorable advertisement went with it. It said, "If a new Jeep vehicle can't take you there, maybe you ought to think twice about going." It was good advice.

The 1980s saw the coming of the XJ two-door and four-door models. These Wagoneers and Cherokees were shorter, narrower, and lighter than their ancestors. Motorists could also switch to four-wheel drive without

The Super Wagoneer became a popular model.

stopping and locking the front axle. "Shift-on-the-fly" was the new game.

Jeep had spent $250 million on this breakthrough vehicle, and it was highly popular. But other carmakers were not just standing by. Soon, strong competition was on the scene—even from other countries. From the United States came the Ford Bronco and, later, the Explorer. Chevrolet, which was part of the huge General Motors Corporation, produced the Blazer.

From Japan came the Suzuki Samurai and the Isuzu Trooper. Toyota's Land Cruiser—another Japanese vehicle—was catching on, too, as were Toyota's 4-Runner and

Nissan's Pathfinder. Great Britain's Land Rover had been around for many years. It grew more popular than ever before. Even Germany's Mercedes-Benz and Italy's Lamborghini companies—which produced some of the fastest and most expensive cars in the world—got into the act with vehicles of their own.

Jeeps still get people into the wild outdoors.

In spite of all this competition, the new XJs repaid Jeep's huge investment. The Cherokee was voted four-wheel-drive car of the year by three different magazines. By 1985, 75 percent of the four-wheel-drive vehicles sold in America were Cherokees.

The XJ series was a triumph. But hard times came to American Motors in the late 1970s and early 1980s. The company tried to solve its problems by joining forces with the French automaker Renault. But the hookup with Renault was not enough to cure the company's ills. Jeep was in deep trouble.

Finally, in 1987, the Chrysler Corporation took over American Motors. The vehicle first designed more than 50 years ago—and built by Bantam, Ford, Willys-Overland, Kaiser, and American Motors—was now to be made by the Jeep and Eagle division of the Chrysler Corporation.

In the years since then, Jeep has regained its place on the road. The one-millionth Jeep XJ rolled off the Toledo, Ohio, assembly line on March 20, 1990. Today **four-by-fours** (4x4s), as four-wheel-drive vehicles are often called, are among the most popular cars in the United States. And they are becoming almost equally popular in other parts of the world.

Today's Jeeps are a far cry from the ones that rolled off the assembly lines during World War II. Heat, air conditioning, and even stereo CD players are all available. Some of

The Cherokee Chief set new standards for Jeep comfort.

the new Jeeps can even automatically tell when to switch from two-wheel drive to four-wheel drive. Others have a super-low gear for pulling and climbing. But for all its improvements, the Jeep has stayed true to its original purpose. It's a classic that keeps on going year after year— wherever you want it to go.

CHAPTER

8

# WILD WILDERNESS BEASTS

Taking vehicles into the wilderness brings responsibilities. After all, without special care, those vehicles can quickly destroy the areas that people want to enjoy.

Years ago, American Motors responded to this by creating scholarships for young environmentalists. Chrysler Corporation's Jeep and Eagle Division has continued the tradition. It has sponsored environmental and safety programs to go with its go-anywhere cars.

Today Jeep supports the U.S. Forest Service's Tread Lightly program. This project teaches drivers how to respect private and public lands while traveling through them. Today, anyone going on a Jeep **jamboree** is required to attend the program.

Jean-Paul Luc—a man who has raced Jeeps in competition—started another interesting program. His Winter Driving School teaches police officers, firefighters, bus drivers, and emergency crews how to

Mountain passes
never stopped a Jeep!

drive in slick winter conditions. And you can guess what vehicles many of the students choose when they tackle winter's worst conditions.

Jean-Paul Luc, of course, is not the only person to race Jeeps. In fact, Jeep races are nothing new at all. Jeeps have been winning off-road rallies and desert races since the 1960s. And before other companies made four-wheel-drive cars, Jeeps had rallies all their own. The first was in France in 1951, where Jeep wheels had replaced horse hooves for delivering milk and cheese.

Jeeps' go-anywhere spirit is very much alive today.

The French Jeep drivers wanted more to do than make deliveries. So they started competing in tests of skill and endurance. Bets were made, and winners grew hungry for more serious challenges. They created their own breakneck race, the Rallye des Cimes. It bounced over a muddy course of rocks, hills, and cliffs. The treacherous course was more fit for mules than humans and took nearly 24 hours to complete.

Twenty entries appeared for the first race. Twelve of the jeeps were crippled during practice alone. Eight cars started the actual race, and only three crossed the finish line. One car plunged off a cliff—luckily, without its driver.

The next year the French Automobile Club tried to ban the dangerous race. Still, the racers won out. Word spread to racing buffs in Chile, Romania, Italy, and the United States. Soon, four-wheel-drive races were taking place in dozens of countries.

Today there are off-road rallies all over the world. Some are as incredible as the cars that run them. The Paris to Dakar rally runs from France all the way to Senegal, on the western edge of Africa. The Paris–Moscow–Beijing rally is just as difficult—perhaps even more so. It covers 10,000 pounding miles and takes almost a month to run.

The race starts in the shadow of the Eiffel Tower and speeds east across Europe. The public roads are closed for

the race, so drivers can go as fast as they dare. The paved roads pretty much end in Moscow. From there it's a battle to cross the Ural Mountains and get to central Asia's grassy plains. Then there's Turkmenistan's Kara Kum desert to cross—before going on past the Chinese border.

The trail then climbs 11,000 feet into the Tien Shan, a system of mountains at the very western edge of China. After this it drops out of the ice and snow into the wasteland of the Taklimakan desert. (Taklimakan, according to race veterans, is the Chinese word for "Once you go in, you never come out!") There is another desert after that called the Gobi, where summertime temperatures soar to 120 degrees Fahrenheit. At the end of the race, there's just a peaceful little drive along the Great Wall of China to the ancient city of Beijing.

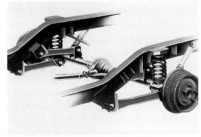

Steep canyons, vast deserts, and distant mountain lakes—whether they

Jeep parts are designed to be tough—and to last.

Jeeps travel sideways when they have to!

are part of the Paris–Moscow–Beijing rally or part of a family's weekend activities—are all grounds for adventures in a Jeep. Two-wheel-drive cars would fall apart just looking at pictures of these places. But for a Jeep, just about anything is possible. In fact, whatever the terrain or the purpose of the trip, one thing is clear. Nothing is ever just another ride when you're riding in a Jeep.

# GLOSSARY

**amphibian** 🚜 An animal or machine that can survive both on land and in the water.

**axle** 🚜 A rod on which a wheel turns; the bar joining the front wheels or back wheels of a vehicle.

**bailout** 🚜 An escape, especially by jumping from a vehicle.

**bug** 🚜 A problem or difficulty.

**Caterpillar tracks** 🚜 Ridged tracks that move in a circle and allow a vehicle to go where wheeled vehicles cannot; often used on earth movers and tanks.

**civilian** 🚜 A person who is not a member of the armed forces.

**David and Goliath** 🚜 Two figures from the Bible; David, a small boy, defeated the giant Goliath by using a slingshot.

**differential** 🚜 Part of the axle of an automobile or other vehicle; its gears allow the outside wheel to turn faster than the inside wheel when the vehicle is going around a corner.

**four-by-four** 🚜 A four-wheel-drive vehicle; often spelled 4x4.

**four-wheel drive** 🚜 A system that sends power from the engine to all four wheels, instead of just the front or rear wheels; this allows vehicles to hold the road better, especially in rain, snow, mud, and similar conditions.

**hub** 🚜 The center of an axle or wheel.

**jamboree** 🚜 A large rally or gathering.

**mortar** 🚜 A small cannon that shoots shells on a high arc or curve.

**orchid** 🚜 A type of plant with remarkable flowers.

**poncho** 🚜 A large piece of cloth with a slit for a person's head to go through; waterproof ponchos are often worn by soldiers, hikers, and campers.

**Quad** 🚜 A four-wheel-drive vehicle.

**rocket** 🚜 A tubelike object that is shot through the air; it is moved forward by the gases that are burned inside the rocket.

**sabotage** 🚜 The destruction of machines and other important equipment by secret forces, usually spies or enemy agents.

**seep** 🚜 A World War II military vehicle, similar to a jeep and designed for use in water.

**snorkel** 🚜 A short tube that brings air to a person or machine under water.

**traction** 🚜 Pulling power; the ability to pull through soft or sticky surfaces.

# FURTHER READING

*Consumer Guide,* editors. *The Weapons of Desert Storm.* New York: NAL/Dutton, 1991.

Dixon, Malcolm. *Land Transportation.* New York: Franklin Watts, 1991.

Hogg, Ivan V. *Modern Military Techniques: Tanks.* London, England: Nomad Publishers, 1985.

Ladd, James D. *Modern Military Techniques: Helicopters.* Minneapolis: Lerner, 1987.

Maynard, Christopher. *War Vehicles.* Minneapolis: Lerner, 1980.

Nicholas, J. *Tracked Vehicles.* New York: Rourke Corp., 1989.

# INDEX